Stocks:

Stock Trading Mastery: Complete Beginner's Guide To Building Riches Through The Stock Market

James Wentworth

Disclaimer Notice:

Table Of Contents

Introduction

When it comes to wealth management many people wonder what is best for their money. Some think of directly investing in a business while others prefer to lock it away in the bank for a long time. However, neither of these options will effectively help you increase your money's worth and for that, you have to consider the Stock Market as your primary choice.

The stock market is a money market where trade takes place on a daily basis. Both buyers and sellers converge either under a single roof or on a single online platform to buy and sell stocks. It includes the purchase and sale of stocks, mutual funds, precious metals and many other instruments. But that is just the tip of the iceberg — in this book we will delve into the depths of a stock market and look at everything that an amateur investor needs to know.

The book has been divided into 9 chapters with each one explaining a particular aspect of the market. My goal is that reading this book will help you to develop into a confident and educated trader. Once you are finished reading, you will be well equipped to reach your personal goal for return on your investment. It's time to take charge of your wealth.

Let's get started!

Chapter 1

About The Stock Market

I thank you for choosing this book and hope you have a good time reading it. In this first chapter of the book, we will look at the basics of the stock market and what you need to know before getting started with stock market investments. No prior knowledge is necessary to begin your investment journey. To do this we will answer a series of important questions that will help define terms and ideas used in stock trading.

What is the stock market?

The stock market is a liquid market where financial instruments are traded on a day-to-day basis. It is a physical or virtual market where both buyers and sellers converge on a daily basis and trade in stocks and other financial instruments.

The Dutch East India Company was the first joint-stock company to regularly sell its stock after its founding in 1602. The sale of these stocks took place on the Amsterdam Exchange and showed a considerable average profit for buyers of around 16%. Due to opportunities in the New World, trading companies based in Europe continued to sell shares into the early 18th century. However, the profit forecasts had been exaggerated and led to a price collapse and the British Bubble Act of 1720, which barred all unauthorized joint-stock companies.

The stock market was not fully revived until 1792 when the New York Stock exchange received its first security. Since then, stock markets have seen a steady growth, both in terms of the number of securities traded and the number of stock exchanges that exist worldwide.

Today, stock markets exist in almost every developed country, as well as many developing countries. Some of the most well known markets besides the New York Stock Exchange include the London Stock Exchange, the Tokyo Stock Exchange (also called Tōshō), the Shanghai Stock

Exchange, Euronext Paris (formerly known as the Paris Bourse) and the Frankfurt Stock Exchange.

Stock markets can be of two types, namely a physical market and a virtual market. A physical market is where buyers and sellers converge to buy and sell stocks on a day-to-day basis. The New York Stock Exchange is the oldest physical stock market in the United States and the most affluent physical stock market in the world. A physical stock market exists in most countries in the world. A virtual market is an online stock market whose popularity rose during the dotcom bubble of the late 1990s.

Advancing technology and the rise in popularity of personal computers allowed for ease of trade via web browser. This led to the existence of new Internet-based companies, increasing stock prices and a boom in trade. The bubble collapsed in 2001, leading to the failure of some of the recently created companies. A few of the surviving companies, however, such as Amazon and eBay, are now stronger than ever.

A good example of a virtual market is the NASDAQ where people can buy and sell stocks through the Internet by creating an online account. It was founded in 1971 as the first electronic stock market. Despite not having a physical location, it is the second largest exchange by market capitalization in the world today and is only super ceded by the New York Stock Exchange. There are now also numerous other virtual exchanged such as Britain's Techmark, for example.

Both physical and virtual markets are quite popular with the former edging out the latter by just a small margin. It is possible for a person to be a part of both these markets at once, as there are no restrictions for how many exchanges you can be part of. Obviously it will be best to start out small and only participate in one or a couple, but your options are endless.

How does the stock market work?

The stock market works on the principle of demand and supply. When there is a demand for a particular stock then its value increases. If there is no demand, then its value decreases. Similarly, if there is a short supply of a stock then its value increases and if there is a lot of supply then its value comes down. This demand and supply is based on how people value the stocks that they hold. If unfavorable news breaks out about a company then everybody will rush to dispose of the stocks that they hold, thereby bringing down its value considerably.

The most famous case is the Stock Market Crash of 1929 which led to the Great Depression. A series of small declines in the market worldwide caused people to panic and eventually led to the selling of around 16 million shares on what is now known as Black Tuesday. As evidenced through history, the stock market crash had a huge impact on world economies and led to a period of widespread poverty. The stability of the stock market has since been of great concern and regulations and precautions are regularly taken to ensure that a similar crash does not happen again, even though it cannot be completely ruled out.

A more recent example on a smaller scale is when Walmart's stock dipped 10% on October 15th, 2015, due to an announcement that the minimum wage would be raised. Stock values are very much in tune with current developments and even small corporate news can effect stock prices greatly.

On the other hand, if there is favorable news about a particular company then people will rush to buy its stocks thereby creating a massive demand. Gold prices, for example, have been known to rally several percentage points in one day. Although it sounds pretty straightforward, it is extremely difficult to predict market trends. It is important to stay up to date with current events and in tune with the market atmosphere. But no matter how careful you are, there will always be some contrarians in the market that will choose to go against the force and end up creating an imbalance. We will talk more about contrarians and other types of investors later on.

The stock market also works on the basis of company reputation and profit margins. The value of a stock can rise or drop after the company announces its results. Investors also appreciate transparency in earnings reports and stocks generally do better when a company is known to be honest in releasing even bad results, than the stocks of a company who will not release results to the public at all.

The many factors contributing to stock value make investment an extremely interesting and multi-faceted endeavour. Research is constantly being conducted to figure out exactly what makes the market tick. Once you have started investing on your own, you will get a feel for the marketplace that will help guide your decisions.

What financial instruments are traded in the stock market?

There are many types of financial instruments that are traded in the stock market. When trading you will never have to worry about running out of options and you will easily be able to diversify your investment portfolio. Right from company shares to foreign exchange to precious metals to electronic funds transfer, there are many types of financial instruments that are traded in the market. We will look at each of these in detail in the chapters to follow.

Who can trade in the stock market?

Anybody willing to invest their money to buy and sell shares of companies or other such financial instruments can invest in the stock market. There is no hard and fast rule that forbids or allows people to invest in the market. The Internet has made it possible for anyone from any country to invest in almost any exchange. Of course there are different tiers of investment and some may be able to invest more than others. We will get into all the details of this later, but if you have the means for it and are of legal age then you can invest. Minors can also invest through a guardian or representative. Groups of people can also pool in money and invest in the market.

Is there a minimum investment to be made?

No. There is no minimum sum required for stock market investments. It is entirely up to you to choose how much you wish to invest. Some people trade within a specified range in order to keep tab of their investments. Some others choose to invest however much they think is best to invest based on what they have at their disposal.

If you are just starting out, you can invest as little as the cost of one single share as there is no minimum share purchase requirement. This means you could spend less than $25 in your first investment. Investment in mutual funds can cost a little more as there is often a minimum purchase requirement. As we will discuss more later on, it is also important to have a budget. Even though you may be dealing with smaller amounts early on, creating the habit of budgeting will be of great help later on when you are dealing with larger sums.

How much can I make from my stock market investments?

The stock market can be a lucrative place for those looking to earn a high margin of income from their investments. It is hard to say how much a person might make from it and will entirely depend on how much has been invested in the first place. That being said, it is also possible for people to invest just a small amount and yet reap a big outcome from it.

The key is to inform yourself about your options and the current market situation and to diversify as much as possible. Diversification options will be pointed out for you throughout this book. The market has been consistently growing despite normal ups and downs. Over the last 100 years the average growth rate of the market has been 10%. If you leverage your choices correctly, you should be guaranteed a return on your investment of at least that average rate, but hopefully you will be able to make even more than that.

How long does it to take to realize gains from the market?

About a month is enough for you to start realizing a gain on your investments. But if you are interested in long term gains then you might have to hold on to the stocks for much longer. Remember that the stock market is generally not a "get rich quick" scheme. While cases do exist where people have hit it big without much investment of time or money, most large investment returns are earned through hard work and over a longer period of time. Most likely you will have to wait a year or two before you even double your money.

There are always two ways of realizing a profit from your stocks. One is where you capitalize on the difference of its face value and the other where you wait for the dividends to be paid out. Capitalizing on the difference of face value takes constant supervision of the ups and downs of the market, as well as a certain amount of prediction ability. Waiting for dividend payout, on the other hand, takes patience.

I hope answering these questions has given you a good foundation to move forward. Knowing some of the history of the stock market, its purposes and its options are all important to your future investments. All these form the various basics of the stock market.

Chapter 2

Getting Started with the Stock Market

When it comes to stock market investments, there are some things that you have to do first in order to start off on the right foot. In this chapter, we will look at the different steps you have to take to get started with your stock market investments. Some of these steps you may have already taken and others may be completely new to you. Following these steps will ensure that you are well equipped to begin your journey.

Get a computer

The first thing you will need is a computer. You have to have a computer system in place which you can use to trade in the market. Some people prefer to use a laptop but a desktop will work best as you can have a dedicated station for it. Make sure that you have a good Internet connection as every second counts in the stock market. Slow Internet might mean missing out on scoring a lucrative deal. You might also need a backup like a dongle that you can use to connect if the Internet is patchy.

Nowadays there are also many options for mobile platforms, such as tablets and smart phones. While using a computer as your main connection to the market, having information readily available on your mobile device is also important. It will make sure that you can stay updated with real time information. Many apps can also be programmed to send you an alert if a certain stock hits a predefined value. Using a mobile device in conjunction with your computer is a smart way to go and the best way to stay connected.

Find a firm

Next, you have to find a firm that will help you trade in the stock market. In order to buy and sell financial securities, you have to be a part of the stock market and not everybody can be a firm to do that. Therefore, you have to find a financial firm that is a member of the stock exchange and trade through their account. These firms will charge you a fee every time that you buy and sell these stocks and you have to understand the fees thoroughly before opening the account.

Make sure to do some research on what each firm offers to find the perfect fit for you. Often an exchange will have a list of firms that trade with them, which helps you to find your options.

Open an account

Next, you have to fill out the forms and open a trading account. You will have to buy and sell stocks through this account alone. Everybody is issued just a single account per firm, but it is possible to hold an account in more than one firm. You will have access to your account on a daily basis.

It is not possible for two people to share an account and each individual has to have their own. For example, you and your spouse cannot have a joint account. If you wish to both trade separately, you must each form your own accounts. Part of the reason for this is that personal information and identification is required. If you wish to take over from someone then you have to notify your company about it first.

Employ a broker

You must next employ a broker. The broker will take care of your account for you and make the investments. The firms that open your trading account will also provide brokering services. There are two types of brokers to pick from. One being full time brokers with the other being part time brokers. Full time brokers will be available to you full time and you don't have to do anything to remain invested in the stock market. They will use your money to make investments for you and you can check the investments every now and then. This is a very laid back and hands off approach to trading. Examples of some full time brokers include Merrill Lynch and TD Ameritrade.

A part time broker on the other hand will have to be supervised and will expect you to do the requisite research. He or she will only buy and sell the shares for you and not do anything more. The former will charge you a hefty sum whereas the latter will charge nominally, so if you are looking for a frugal option, a part time broker is the way to go. Part time brokers, also called discount brokers, are abundant in the market. This approach is very hands-on and requires your constant involvement in the process. You have probably heard of Charles Schwab and Scottrade, to name just a few examples.

Remember that each of these companies has something slightly different to offer. TD Ameritrade, for example, does not have a minimum deposit amount, whereas Scottrade has a minimum deposit of $2,000. For some people this might not make a difference, but if you are looking to start investing with smaller amounts, Scottrade might not be the best broker option for you. Make sure to do your research before choosing a broker.

Familiarize yourself with software

Next, you have to familiarize yourself with the software. The software is what will allow you to buy and sell the stocks. The software is generally an interface that is downloaded from the company's website and installed on your system which directly communicates with the exchange. You can have someone help you out if you are not familiar with it, or not particularly tech-savvy. Once done, you have to learn how to login to your account and what you have to do to buy and sell the stocks and other instruments.

Don't be shy when exploring your online platform. Make sure to check out all the different options offered before you start using it. Most brokers will also have a hotline you can call for assistance if you should need help. Some companies also offer live chat options within their platform as well.

Additionally, companies will often have an app available for your phone or mobile device. Your login on the computer and on your smart device is the same. This is a great addition to use if you want to stay connected to the market while you are on the go.

Create a watch-list

You can create a watch list for yourself if you like. A watch list is one where you list out all the different stocks that you will be buying and selling. Having a constant update of their prices will help you make the right choices for yourself. This is especially practical for mobile use.

You can create multiple watch lists if you like but must understand that prices vary on a second to second basis and trying to switch between watch lists might only cause you to lose out on money.

However, there are cases where multiple watch lists may be helpful. For example, you might want to group your investments by type. Long term investments could go on one list — these you are not likely to sell on a whim or check every minute of the day — and short term investments could go on another — these you will be checking quite frequently, as the right moment to buy or sell can change very quickly. You could also create a list for each financial instrument that you are investing with. In this way precious metals might be on a different list than mutual funds. The options with watch lists are abundant.

You will also be able to see how many buyers and sellers have currently lined up for the stock. This will help you decide whether or not you want to buy or sell a share. If it looks like many people are selling a certain stock, you may want to hold on a bit and wait for the stock price to come back up again. If many are buying a stock, this could be an indication that the price is currently favorable and it would be best to buy now before the cost goes up. There is no written rule to follow, but gaining experience and a feel for the market will be your best guide.

Buy

Next, you have to start buying the stocks and other financial instruments. As was mentioned before, you have to login to your account and place a bid for the stocks you wish to buy. Make sure that you have your payment method set up ahead of time. Most brokers require direct deposit for any purchase in stock. If you are unable to set up direct deposit, payment by check is also possible. This, however, takes longer, which is a disadvantage when wanting to buy and sell quickly.

Once you have purchased a stock, you have to wait to see if it is approved and you have the stocks in your account. It generally takes just a few seconds. But if you are bidding for an IPO or initial public offering then you might have to wait for a week to a few weeks before being allotted the stocks.

Buying IPO stocks means that you are not trading, but rather buying the first shares made available by a company. Often you will not know the amount of shares you receive until after the IPO has been completed. It is a great option if you want to invest in a new company, but there is no way of knowing how the stock value will hold up once it is on the market and there is no stock history for you to study to help make your decision. For these reasons IPO purchases are better for the experienced trader.

Sell

Once you have the stocks you can either hold them or sell them. If you wish to sell them then you must give the call through your account. You will be able to see how many people want the stocks and how many are already trying to sell. It might take a few seconds to minutes for all your stocks to be disposed of. You will get a notification on your cell phone or email once they have been successfully sold. If you have made a profit from it then you will be notified about the same. If you have a loss then you will be notified as well.

Always make sure to double-check your numbers before selling. An error in decimal point or other calculation could lead to losses when you thought you were in for a good profit, or it could cause you to hang on to a stock that would be profitable to sell. Either way, it is also important to check your numbers twice before you act on them.

Repeat

Some of your investments may be long term and not require sale for a long period of time. Other investments you will be buying and selling possibly even within the same day. In this case you have to keep the process of buying and selling stocks and other securities going in a loop. There is no limit to how many stocks you can buy and sell on a daily basis. You can buy and sell to your heart's content.

However, it is important to keep track of how much you are spending on the stocks. Many people over spend without realizing it and struggle to withdraw the money later. While the trade in the stock market is by definition not gambling, it can have the same feel. If you tend to enjoy gambling and getting caught up in the moment, it is especially important for you to set a monetary spending limit for yourself at the beginning of the day and have your month carefully budgeted out. This will keep you from biting off more than you can chew.

Record

You have to record all your transactions. This is especially crucial for all those that have recently started investing in stocks. Looking back at older transactions will help you know where you are going wrong and what you have to do to avoid the same mistakes.

If you are using an online platform, looking up your trade history is quite easy. However, your trade history will only go so far back. You may find it advantageous to keep a separate diary either electronically on the computer, or handwritten in a ledger. This way you know you will always have the information readily available.

Altogether the steps are quite simple: make sure that you have a device capable of a fast Internet connection, pick your firm(s) and broker(s)and start to buy and sell on a continual basis after careful consideration, budgeting and record keeping. These actions form the different steps that you have to take in order to start investing in the stock market.

Chapter 3

Stock Trading Basics

The most traded securities in the stock market are stocks. Stocks or shares refer to a share in a company's ownership. They represent in sum the net asset value of a company. The idea of owning equity in a company is by no means new and has been around since the Roman Empire, if not earlier.

If you were to buy shares of a company, then you would be buying a stake in its ownership. But of course it will not make you a majority owner and your name will not appear on the list of board of directors. It does, however, give you the right to vote in matters of the company. The number of authorized shares issued by a company is up to them and varies greatly. A start-up company, for example, may only issue a few thousand shares. A company like Amazon, on the other hand, has issued 5 and a half billion shares. In most cases the shares that you will hold will be just a fraction of what is being offered to the public by the company.

A stock or share is a safe bet for some as it provides the investor with a lot of flexibility. The investment amount and timing is all left up to the buyer. He or she will not have to rush to make a decision on whether to keep or dispose of them.

Stocks are of two types and they are discussed in the following.

Preference stocks

Preference stocks are those that are mostly held by the top-level employees of the company or by large investors. They might not be floated for public buying in the stock market, unless one of the holders decides to do so and it is permitted by the company. Preference stocks help the holder receive a fixed dividend on a monthly basis. They will also be considered first in case a company winds up and will be paid in full or part depending on how much money remains with the company at the end after settling all its debts. These debts include bonds, which we will discuss in more detail later on.

The benefit of preference or preferred shares is that they have a higher fixed dividend return. Preference share owners, however, will have no say in the employment of board of directors of the company and do not hold voting rights. The person might also not be able to transfer these stocks to another person. The shares can be described as a cross between a bond and a stock and have no minimum purchase price just as common stocks.

Another thing to consider is that most companies hold the right to buy back preferred shares at any time for a premium. Preference stocks are also usually a small percentage of the total share amount when compared with common shares. For example, of Amazon's 5 and a half billion stocks, only half a billion are preference stocks. The other 5 billion are common stocks, which we will look at next.

Ordinary or common stocks

The other type of shares is known as ordinary or common shares. These are what are generally bought and sold in the stock market. You don't have to be part of the top brass of the company or a large investment firm to own these.

Ordinary stocks do not entitle the owners to a fixed dividend on a monthly basis. However, they will have a say in the employment of the board of directors of the company as they give you voting rights. Ordinary stocks are thought to be safe bets as the owner can transfer, buy, or sell them at their disposal. As the name suggests, common shares are far the majority between the two types of stock.

It is possible for a person to hold both these types of shares at once. In fact, it is important to have a diverse portfolio. As a beginner you will most likely start with common shares, but don't think that preferred shares are off the table once you have gained some experience in the market.

Types of markets

There are two types of stock market situations namely the bull market and the bear market. Both these are radically different from each other and are both based on the market forces that govern them. The bear market represents a continual decrease in stock prices over a long period of time and the bull market represents a continual increase.

A bear market is better known as a seller's market. It is named after how the bear attacks its prey. Just like the bear swoops down to embrace its prey, the bear market is a downward market. People generally prefer to short sell their stocks so that they can save themselves some losses. The bearish market generally comes into being when the economy of a country is bad and recession is on. Most investors dread the bearish market and prefer to wait until it passes by, but contrarian traders generally enjoy purchasing stock during a bearish market and many have done so successfully.

A bear market is especially dangerous as it can lead to a perpetual downward spiral. People are selling their stock and contributing to a general feeling of pessimism in the market, which can then lead to more people selling stock, turning it into a vicious cycle. This cycle is sometimes not broken until sentiment reaches rock bottom and buying stock again is the only thing left to do. This is often called "capitulation."

The bull market, on the other hand, is better known as a buyer's market. The bull market is one where the prices of stocks are rising. It is named after the bull and how it flings its prey into the air. Stock prices will steadily rise in the bull market. This type is ideal for most investors as they will be able to freely buy and sell shares while making a consistent profit.

Obviously there are times when buying in a bear market and selling in a bull market are profitable as well. Careful research of stock prices and being in tune with the mood of the current market are vital to understanding when this is the case. For example, sometimes certain stocks will not follow the market mood and remain bearish while the market stays bullish and vice versa. So it is wrong to generalize for all stocks and you must look into them individually.

You may be wondering how the terms "bear" and "bull" became associated with the trade market. Documents show the use of these words as far back as 18th century England. "Bear" originates from an old expression that said you should not sell a bear skin before you had killed the animal. This is very similar to our modern day expressions of "counting your chickens before your eggs are hatched" and "putting the cart before the horse." It started being associated with the market when people began to sell stocks with the intent of buying them later at a more profitable price.

The term bull started to be used shortly after the term bear. Its origins aren't quite as clear, but throughout history the bull has always symbolized strength, power and fertility. All of these qualities are what you want to see in a strong market.

To continue with animal terminology in the stock market, a person who is willing to take a big risk and starts dealing during the bullish phase is known as a pig, whereas, someone afraid of investing or taking risks is known as a chicken. We hope that through reading this book, you will be known as a wise fox, rather than a pig or a chicken when it comes to the market. As with many things in life, balance is key in your investments and you do not want to be known as a pig or a chicken.

What causes stock price fluctuations?

As was mentioned earlier, the stock market operates on the principle of demand and supply. If there is a lot of demand for a stock then its price will remain high, as there won't be enough to distribute to all. On the other hand, if there are a lot of stocks floating in the market and less demand for it then its price will drop. You can observe the same principle in the fluctuation of everyday items that you purchase, such as a gallon of gas, or a gallon of milk.

It is difficult to predict which stocks might remain high and which might collapse as it depends on the mood of the market. To get an idea and a feel for stock price flexibility, it would be good for you to pick several stocks of well-known companies to observe throughout the day and over a period of time. You can learn a lot from observation alone without having to spend a single dollar.

Gains from stocks

There are two types of gains that can be had from stocks and they are: profits and dividends.

Profits are what you are left with when you sell stocks in the stock market for a higher rate than what you paid for them. Say for example you buy a stock at $50 and then sell it at $60. You are left with a profit of $10 from the transaction. Your profit will also multiply with the number of stocks that you sell at this rate. If you had 10 of these shares, your total profit would be $100. This amount will vary depending on the value of the stock at the buying and the selling stage. The choice of when to sell is entirely up to you.

The other income from stocks is known as the dividend. Dividend is a sum of money that is paid to the stockholder at regular intervals, mostly at the beginning of the month. For common shares there is no fixed amount that is usually paid and it depends on how many stocks the person has in the company. For preferred stocks, you receive a fixed rate dividend that is generally higher than that of a common share. In both cases, the bigger the share the higher the dividend!

It is possible for you to get both of these returns from the same stocks. Say for example you bought a stock on February 23rd for $20. The company announced a dividend of $1 per share on 1st march. You were paid the dividend on the 15th and you sold the shares for $22 on the 15th. You will remain with both the dividend and the profit from the same transaction. In this case you will have made $3 for every share that you owned for only 3 weeks.

As an amateur, it is best for you to observe the market for some time before making investments. You might have to look at how certain stocks are performing before making an investment.

Most brokers allow you to create an account without actually investing any shares right at the beginning. If you do this, you will be able to use your watch list to keep track of stock movement without needing to spend any money. This is one great tool that will help you in getting a feel for the market.

Once you are logged in to your account you will be able to see that there are stocks listed under different categories and you should pick the top 5 from each one to follow. You have to diversify your portfolio and not have your stocks in the same category of industry. For example, you should buy a few stocks from the banking category and some from the IT category etc.

Don't be overwhelmed at first if you are unable to make hefty profits from your investments. It will get better with time and you will be able to ring in substantial profits with time. Remember that trading in the stock market is a journey where you are constantly learning. Staying up to date with current news and sites like Forbes can also be very helpful in your learning experience. Investment takes patience and you will need to persevere to see results.

Worldwide market

The stock market is a worldwide market and people can buy and sell stocks from anywhere in the world, from the New York Stock Exchange to the Hong Kong Stock Exchange. But, you will have to be a part of the country's stock exchange. For example, you can be a resident of New York and buy and sell on the NYSE but be based in China.

The only thing that will hinder your trade is the difference in time zones.

Another thing to be aware of is that not all brokers provide services in all markets. If you are looking to make a certain foreign investment, it is best to contact your broker first to see if they offer this service. If they do not offer it, they may be able to connect you with a broker in the country that you are wishing to invest in and you may have to create another account with that broker.

You also need to educate yourself about the different regulations and taxes that may apply when transferring money from your foreign profits back to your local bank account. Trade in different world markets can be very lucrative, but it does require an additional set of knowledge.

Chapter 4

Options Trading Basics

We looked at the basics of the stock market in the previous chapter and hope you have understood it. We will now move on to options trading. Options refer to financial proposals that are made by the seller to the buyer for an underlying security that he wishes to dispose of.

Let us first look at a generic example to understand the conccpt better. Let's say I have with me a cellphone that I wish to sell for $100. You agree to buy it under the condition that you pay $50 to reserve it and take possession of it after paying the remaining amount in a week's time. During the weeks that follow, you find out that the phone belonged to Brad Pitt and its actual market value is $500. You can immediately buy it and settle the deal. I cannot raise the price now and will have to sell it at the agreed price.

On the other hand, you find out that the phone is being overcharged as the company has stopped producing the model. In that case, you can refuse to buy it but will have to forgo the $50 that you paid as advance.

Now let us look at a real example. Say I have 100 shares of a company that I wish to sell at $20 each. I make the proposal to you and you agree to it under the condition that you will only pay $500 to reserve the stocks for you. I agree on the condition that you have to pay the remainder to me within 2 weeks.

Now in the 2 weeks that follow, two different things can happen. First, you might find out that the stocks are great and are being offered to you at a great discount. You can immediately settle it and buy the shares at the agreed plan. Here, I can't raise the price of the stocks and have to sell it at the agreed price.

On the other hand, you might find out that the stocks are actually pretty bad and are being sold at a very high price. Here, you can refuse to buy the stocks from me and not pay the remainder. However, you will have to part with the advance money that you have paid.

That is the "option" that you have. Many people prefer this type as they have the chance to save on a lot of money and also have ample time to decide whether they want to buy a stock or not. In a sense, options allow you the ability to see the future before completely committing to a deal, while retaining the current stock price. The only amount that is at risk is your initial down payment.

Most stock options require you buy 100 shares at any point in time. Here, in the first case, you are going to remain with a profit. Say you find out that the shares are actually worth $30 each. You have to pay another $1500 to buy the stocks. Once you do, you will have 100 stocks worth $30 each in your possession. The profit that you make from it can be calculated by subtracting the final sum from what you paid for the stocks which in this case is $3,000-$2,000 = $1,000. Generally, you have to take into consideration the commission as well, which will depend on the financial firm and is either subtracted from your profit, or charged to you in cases where you show no profit.

The $20 per share is known as the call price and the $30 is the strike price. The investor will always have a strike price in mind while making an investment.

There are two main types of options and they are as follows:

American options

American options are those where the option owner has the chance of settling the underlying stocks on or before the specified period. There is no need to wait until the maturity period for the options has come by. The person can short sell it if they like. This is the most common type of options that are traded all over the world.

American options are mainly sold on futures exchanges. Interestingly, the first modern futures exchange was started in Japan at the outset of the 18th century. A futures exchange is an exchange specifically for the trade of futures contracts. We will talk a little more about futures under commodities.

European option

European options are the other type of options. European options will require the buyer to settle the deal only at the time of maturity and not before. So even if a lucrative phase comes in between, he will be forced to hold on to the options and not sell them. European options are used mainly in over-the-counter trades, meaning a direct trade that takes place outside of an exchange between two parties and without the use of a third party. This type is not popular at all and many people prefer to not invest in such options.

American and European options form the two most common types of options that you can invest with in the stock market. The former is much more popular than the latter and what many investors prefer for their investments.

While American and European options are the most common, they are not the only types of options. Another category known as exotic options includes all those that do not pertain to the previously mentioned ones. The previous types of options are generally called plain vanilla options and everything that is apart from them is exotic options. Some of these options include Bermuda options, Canary options and Evergreen options. All of these have slight variations of use. The Bermuda option, for example, allows you to settle the deal at a number of pre-designated points in time, instead of just at the end as with the European option.

Note that the names European and American options, etc., have nothing to do with geography and are just names of the options. All of these options are available around the world and are not restricted to a certain country.

Apart from these there is also a classification into short term and long term options. Short-term options are those that you settle within a short period of time whereas long terms are those that come with a long term settling period. Obviously there are benefits and drawbacks of both. Short term options allow you more flexibility and the ability to try a greater number of options. Long-term options, on the other hand, provide stability.

Why choose options?

Options are a safe bet for starters, as they will know how to predict market conditions and make use of the future trend of a stock. They are also a great learning tool, because they force you to watch the market carefully and decide when the best time is to make the deal with the seller. Doing this will give you a good feel for the market and boost your confidence when investing directly in stocks.

Another reason to choose options is that the level of risk involved is lesser than it is in the share market. The only amount of money you are putting at risk is your down-payment amount, whereas with normal stocks your entire investment is immediately at risk. This is especially beneficial for short-term options. When purchasing stocks, you may have to wait a long time to see any reward. The stock price could drop several times before it finally comes back up to give you a profit. But if you have chosen the stock via option and it drops, you have the chance to step out and invest elsewhere, while only losing your initial down-payment. If you don't have the time to wait for the stock price to come back up, then options are definitely the way to go.

However, you must also account for the downside of things. The options market is great no doubt but you have to understand that it is not thoroughly liquid. You might have to wait for a while before being able to successfully sell your stocks. This is especially tricky if you have chosen a European option, because it only allows you to make the deal at the predesignated point in time. The entire time leading up to that is merely a waiting game.

Chapter 5

Forex Trading Basics

The next type of investment is known as forex trading. Forex refers to the foreign exchange market and is also known as FX or currency market. It is, by volume, the greatest trading platform in the world. As we know, no two countries can have the same currencies except by agreement and most everybody has their own individual ones.

The foreign exchange market emerged in the 1970s after lifting of regulation through what was known as the Bretton Woods system. This allowed for currencies to have variable rather than fixed rates. Most transactions through Forex are done by bank dealers, who allow you to purchase one currency by paying with another. Forex is open 24 hours a day on business days, which makes it a very different animal than the stock market exchanges. Due to its international nature it also has very few regulations.

Forex trading refers to a type of trading where the investor buys and sells foreign currencies. So, if I were an investor in the stock market then I would buy the currency of a country and sell it at a later time to ring in a profit. This can become very profitable, as the value of currency is an extremely liquid thing.

You have to know that there are both strong currencies and weak ones. Strong currencies are those that have a great value in the market owing to a strong economy whereas weak ones are those that belong to countries that are not economically stable. Strong currencies are also known as hard currencies and weak currencies are often called soft currencies. To achieve hard currency status, a currency must demonstrate stability and strength over a long period of time. Hard currencies in the past have included the US Dollar, the Swiss Franc and the Japanese Yen, to name a few. Soft currencies, on the other hand, are often found in developing countries and are known to fluctuate greatly in value.

So, an investor will look to buy a strong currency in exchange for a weak one thereby boosting his chances of making a big profit from it. It is important for investors to keep track of markets as currency prices rise and fall on a daily basis. They have to check if the currency of their choice has risen or dropped in value. If it has risen, then the investor will decide to sell the currency to bring in the profit. If the value has dropped then the investor will wait until it rises back up.

You can easily find current exchange rates online. Most brokers will also offer real-time information in regard to currencies. Just as you can have a watch list for stocks or options, you can also create a watch list for currencies that you are interested in.

Major currencies

There are 8 major currencies in the world based on their country's economy. They are said to be great currencies to buy, as their value will be quite high at any given point in time, in comparison to other currencies. These all fall in the hard currency category.

US Dollar

The US dollar is one of the strongest currencies in the world. The US economy is quite stable which allows the currency to remain stable as well. Although there can be a few fluctuations, it will not be too drastic or fast. Since the

1970s, when the US Dollar Index (or USDX) was initiated at a value of 100,000, its highest rate has been at 164.72 in 1985 and its lowest value was at 70.698 in 2008. This type of stability will allow the investor sufficient time to make a decision on whether or not they want to trade in the currency. The US Dollar is currently the number one most traded currency by value in the world.

Canadian Dollar

The Canadian dollar is the next most preferred currency to deal with in foreign exchanges. Just like the US dollar, the Canadian dollar is also quite stable. Both currencies are traded on a day-to-day basis and make for lucrative choices. The Canadian dollar (or CAD) has the 7th highest trade rate by value in the world.

United Kingdom Pound Sterling

The pound sterling (or GBP) was once the most influential currency in the world. It is the oldest currency in the world that is still in use today and dates back to the 8th century. One GBP has consistently been worth more than one USD, but it ranks 4th on the list of most traded currencies. There is no doubt that it will continue to remain quite high on the list of currencies to pick while engaging in foreign trade.

Euro

The Euro is the currency for 19 countries in the European Union. It was introduced in non-physical form in 1999and then physically in 2002. The old currencies of the country, such as the German Mark, where slowly phased out in order to make way for the Euro. When it was introduced it was meant to have the same value as the USD. It has since fluctuated in both directions, but has remained largely steady. The Euro is just as powerful as the pound or dollar and is accepted in most parts of Europe. It is the second most traded currency by value in the world.

Swiss Franc

The Swiss Franc in particular is quite strong as well. It is legal tender in Switzerland and Lichtenstein, where it was introduced at the end of the 18th century. The Swiss Franc is widely considered to be a very safe investment with little to no inflation. It ranks 6th overall in the most traded currencies in the world.

Australian Dollar

The Australian dollar is said to be very strong and many old hands prefer to exchange it with a weak currency. Australia has had a stable economy for quite some time. Combine that with low interest rates and little regulation and the

Australian dollar is a great choice. It is currently ranked 5th in the world's most traded currencies, right behind the British pound.

New Zealand Dollar

The New Zealand dollar, also called the Kiwi, was introduced in 1967and is nearly as powerful as the Australian dollar. It is currently ranked number 10 among the world's most traded currencies.

Japanese yen

The Japanese yen is the only Asian currency that is considered to be strong. It was created in the late 19th century in order to keep up with other currencies in the world and replaced the traditionally used Tokugawa coinage. The Yen ranks 3rd in the world's top traded currencies, behind the USD and the EUR. It is an excellent opportunity to invest in the Asian side of the world.

Pairing

When it comes to pairing currencies, you have to always pair a strong one with a weak one. You have to pick two extremes where one is really strong and the other quite weak. You have to look at currency pairs that are doing well and then decide to buy them.

A currency pair is made up of a base currency and a quote currency, with the base currency being the one you are buying and the quote currency being the one you are selling. For example, if you are wanting to sell USD (your quote currency) and buy EUR (your base currency), then you will need to know how many USD it will take to buy one EUR. If EUR/USD= 0.75, that would mean that it takes 75 US cents to purchase one Euro.

Remember that you will always first use your local currency to buy another one. So, you have to exchange it for something that is lower in value so that you remain with a lot more. This would be true in the example we gave above. Then, you exchange the same for a strong currency and then again with a weak one and so on. The idea is to remain with a profit once all the currencies have been exchanged and you once more end up with your local currency.

Over the counter

Most currency exchanges happen over the counter; this means that pink sheets are issued which carry the value of the currencies. Pink sheets are named after the color they were originally written on, but today all the term means is a daily publication of bid-ask stock quotations. The investor does not have to shell out the money each time, especially if the currencies are going to be bought and sold within the same day. He or she will exchange their pink sheets for the profits that they have garnered.

Keep in mind, though, that the pink sheets are a quote and are not the actual currency. It is always best to double check the amount given on your pink sheet, to make sure that the quote is accurate and up to date.

24 hour market

One of the biggest advantages of the forex market is that it is open 24 hours a day except on weekends. This means that you can buy and sell currencies whenever you like, as the market will not close. Physical stock markets have shorter hours. The New York Stock Exchange, for example, is only open Monday through Friday from 9:30 am to 4:00 pm EST. Other countries' exchanges also have specific hours, which can be hard to follow due to time change differences. For this reason, the 24 hour forex market is especially advantageous if you are trading with foreign currencies in different time zones. When you are dealing with these types of currencies then you can stay up and match with their timings.

Liquidity

The forex market is extremely liquid. This means that you will be able to buy and sell foreign currencies with ease and will not have to put in too much effort to find the right person to buy or sell the currency to. Liquidity also means that the market will remain stable despite quick turnaround times and ease of purchasing. In fact, it is this very reassuring quality that makes many first time investors pick foreign exchange.

Transaction Costs

The transaction costs involved in foreign exchange are quite low. You need not worry about having to deal with many middle men, as there will only be a few and those are manageable.

The reason for this is that there are generally no exchange fees, regulatory fees, or data fees. The only fee you may encounter is a commission from forex brokers. There are three different types of commissions — fixed spread, variable spread and a fixed percentage commission, with the spread being the difference between the bid price and the ask price. Make sure to figure out which one of these will best suit your needs before settling on a broker.

These aspects form the various components of the foreign exchange market. As you can see, there are both positives and negatives of forex trading. While there is much less regulation than trading at a stock exchange, you also need to be constantly plugged in to the current rates and economic climates. Knowledge of different cultures is also very beneficial. Overall, think of forex trading as a short term investment option with quick turnaround time. For long term investments you will need to look elsewhere.

Chapter 6

Precious Metals Basics

The next type of stock market investment is known as precious metals investment. As you know, precious metals command a high price in the market and you can ring in a big profit by exchanging them for currency. There are many types of precious metals such as gold, silver and platinum and all of these are individually traded in the precious metal markets.

Gold

Gold is the most traded precious metal in the world. It can be found on almost every continent in the world and is most prolific in South Africa and India. It has been used as a substitute for money throughout history and has never completely lost its value. Many currencies throughout time have been based on gold and the last to change to a flat currency was the Swiss Franc, which had been backed up by a 40% gold reserve up until 2000. Even now there is still a movement to restore the gold reserve percentage of the Swiss Franc.

Abbreviated as AU, gold is a rare metal. It finds its place in jewelry making and other arts due to its beauty and ease of sculpting and also in the industrial business due to its ability to conduct electricity and resistance to rust and deterioration. Gold is also used in the food and fashion industry, thereby making it one of the most widely accepted precious metals in the world still today.

Gold is so desired, that throughout history there have been numerous "gold rushes" whenever a new gold deposit was found. These have taken place in many different countries in the world, including the United States, Canada, Brazil, Australia and South Africa.

Since 1970, the net value of gold against the USD has grown by almost 1,000%, making gold one of the most long-term stable investments available on the market. The benchmark for the world's gold standard is the London Gold Fixing, which has been taking place since 1919. There are currently 11 participants in the fixing, which happens twice daily and determines the gold value for the day for the London bullion market and serves as guide for the entire world.

Gold is generally traded in the form of coins or biscuits (also called bars). It is also a good idea for you to buy gold jewelry, as it will increase in value over time. The value of gold is measured through karats. 24 is said to be the purest and also the thinnest. So, it is not possible to make jewelry out of gold alone and other materials like bronze and zinc get used, which cause the value of the piece to drop.

So, if you are looking for pure gold then it is best for you to pick coins or bars as opposed to jewelry. But you can also pick 22 karat gold pieces that will be quite precious nonetheless.

There are quite a few companies that can help you with your gold investment such as Apmex, Regal Assets and Jim Bullion, just to name a few. Different firms can be easily found and researched on the Internet. Be sure to double check that you are paying a current asking price when investing in gold.

There can be many investors that choose to hold on to a lot of gold for a long time and then sell all of it at once thereby reducing the metal's value. Such practise is common all over the world, which makes many investors abandon buying gold.

Gold can also be bought over the counter much like foreign currency. But since it is held for a long time, many prefer to settle the value before holding it.

Silver

Silver is a precious metal that is quite popular all over the world owing to its sheen and the many places where it gets used. Silver coins and biscuits are traded in the market also as jewelry. Pure silver is better referred to as Sterling silver.

Silver, however, is not as pricey or worth as much as gold. Its prices will not fluctuate as drastically as gold owing to lesser demand and more availability. Silver has played second fiddle to gold as far back as Roman times, when the worth of gold outweighed silver by 12.5 to 1. Since the 19th century the gold to silver ratio has risen drastically and in 2015 it was 65.2 to 1 in the US. Regardless of the ratio, the value of silver has been known to track the value of gold.

Silver is used in jewelry and also the industrial business in applications such as silverware, electronics and even medicine. It remains in demand all through the year, which causes its value to remain high. Silver can be found throughout the world, but the most prominent producers are in North and South America and Australia.

Silver is generally bought in bulk to constitute for a bigger profit margin. The value of both gold and silver rises during sporting events where gold and silver medals are awarded.

Most firms that offer gold investments will also offer silver investments at the same time, but there are also companies that specialize in silver such as the Silver Wheaton Corporation. Once again, it is easy to find a company to invest with on the Internet or through your broker.

Platinum

Platinum is another precious metal that is traded in the market on a regular basis. Platinum is possibly the most precious of all three metals and also the shiniest. It does not have the same history as gold and silver, as it was not discovered until the early 18th century. It is also much rarer than other precious metals and the majority of platinum mined today comes from South Africa.

Platinum is widely used in the jewelry industry where it has become popular in wedding bands and as a strong diamond setting, among other things. It also has a number of industrial uses due to its high corrosion resistance which include everything from catalytic converters to dentistry equipment.

The price of platinum is higher than that of gold owing to its exchange value and to the fact that it is 5 times rarer than gold. Only in extremely poor market conditions has it been known to drop below the price of gold.

Rather than buying physical platinum, many traders rather choose to buy exchange-traded funds, or ETFs, or to invest in platinum mines. Both are good options if you are not wanting to buy physical platinum. If you prefer purchasing the actual commodity, most companies that offer gold and silver will also offer platinum.

Palladium

There are also some other precious metals that are now doing well in the market owing to the scarcity of the other metals. One of them includes palladium, which is a great metal to invest with.

Palladium is an even more recent trading option than platinum, as it was not discovered until the beginning of the 19th century. Palladium does not have as many industrial uses as gold, silver and platinum, but it is known for being used in catalytic converters and it is also used as an alloy to produce white gold, which is very popular today. The majority of palladium is mined in South Africa and in Russia.

You will be able to ring in a big profit if you trade in palladium and will probably make for a better choice than gold. Make sure to check your exchange for palladium, as it is not readily available everywhere.

Silver, platinum and palladium are all white metals yet vary in price and value. You can hold both silver and platinum if you like and in fact, all three metals to enhance your investment portfolio.

Consistent growth

It is known that precious metals rise in value over time. If you are to buy some now, then its price will not remain the same after a few years and it would have increased considerably. Although there can be a few stagnant periods, it will not continue that way for long. Because of this, precious metals can be counted on as an excellent long term investment option. Many people chose IRAs that are backed by precious metals for this exact reason.

Universal trade

You can universally trade in precious metals and there is no limit to where and when you cannot buy and sell them. For example, you can buy gold in the Middle East and then sell it in the US and ring in a profit. Gold will be much cheaper in the Middle East and you will have the chance to buy more. Wherever you chose to buy your gold, whether from a US firm or an Asian firm, make sure that you compare the current gold rates of numerous countries to make sure that you are getting a good deal.

Illiquid bullion

Bullion is the name given to the gold and silver market, specifically when dealing with bulk precious metals in bar and ingot form. One point of distinction to note here is that the precious metal market is slightly illiquid. This means that you will have to wait for some time before your precious metals are absorbed into the market.

This is a big difference from forex trading, which is extremely liquid. With precious metals you have to plan in advance and know when to dispose of your stock. You cannot plan it overnight and have to put some thought into it before disposing of your stock. Precious metals are a long term investment.

Certificates

Now you might wonder as to how you will stock up on all these precious metals and whether it is a safe bet to haul them up at home. After all, all of the precious metals are quite heavy and would cost a good bit to have shipped to your address. Once at home, you would also probably want some sort of safe for storage, which can also become expensive and add to the liability of your insurance.

Don't worry, though, because not many people actually take physical custody of these metals owing to the previous stated concerns. They prefer to get certificates that carry the value of the precious metals on them, while the precious metal itself remains in storage with the firm you chose to invest with. You can exchange the certificates for gold at a later date or you can also give it to someone. Most brokers will issue certificates.

Options

Gold options are quite popular, as they will help both the buyer and seller. The seller will have the chance to make part profit through the booking sum while the buyer will wait for the price of it to rise. This creates a win-win situation, as the seller does not have to wait as long to make a profit off his gold and the buyer does not have to pay full price. Options are in fact a better bet than buying precious metals directly from the market. You will have the chance to command a better price for what you have in your possession.

These items form the various aspects of the precious metals market. As you can see, precious metals are excellent investment options and we have just scratched the surface. If you look further there are even more precious metals and gems that can be invested in, from rhodium to rubies.

Chapter 7

Commodities Trading Basics

We looked at precious metal trading in the previous chapter and now, we will look at commodities.

Commodities refer to everyday products that you use at home. Commodity trading has been around since ancient times. The simplest form, of course, would be direct trade without interchange of money. Before the introduction of currency this would have been the only way to conduct trade. In fact, the Amsterdam Stock Exchange, which is believed to be the first stock exchange in history, was founded for commodity trading in the 17th century, which demonstrates the important of commodity trading to a country's economy.

For our modern purposes today, commodities are traded just like any other financial securities as their prices fluctuate on a day-to-day basis. There are many categories of commodities and some of them are described in the following.

Food/ perishables

The first and foremost traded commodities in the market are food. This refers to perishables that are used on a daily basis universally. It includes vegetables such as potatoes and onions, cocoa, corn, wheat, barley etc. People bet on what their value will be in the future and hold on until the value reaches. Once it does, they quickly dispose of it to ring in a profit.

In order to stay in touch with food commodity pricing you have to understand agriculture. Drought or hail can seriously impact food commodities. Prices can also cause farmers to store their crops rather than immediately selling them, which can also impact stocks.

The value of perishables also varies depending on its use. For example, during Christmas, the value of cocoa might surge owing to an increase in the production of baked goods. Similarly, some seasons might cause an increase in the demand for certain other food commodities. You have to understand how it is affected in order to predict the rise and fall in prices in a better way.

Food commodity prices can change even throughout the course of a day, so it is very important for you to stay connected. If you have watch lists set up on your broker platform, creating a separate list just for food commodities would be wise.

Livestock

Livestock is also traded in the market. Livestock includes the likes of sheep, cows etc. Pork and lamb are also traded. These are live animals that are bet on and the buyer will predict a price that these might reach in the future.

The pricing for agricultural products impacts not only traders, but also farmers. Just as with food commodities, if livestock prices are low, farmers may hold off on selling their herd, which would further impact the price. Once again, being in tune with the current economy and the state of agriculture is very important.

Metals

Besides the precious metals we already discussed, other metals such as copper, iron and zinc are also traded on a day-to-day basis. These metals are generally used in industries thereby increasing their value through several folds.

You have to keep an eye on the news to know if a particular metal is good to invest in. If an industry that requires the use of copper is booming it will greatly affect the commodity price. The same goes for all materials that are used in production, so be sure to keep an eye on flourishing sectors of the economy.

Chemicals

Chemicals are also traded in the market on a regular basis. These can include chemicals such as sulfur and acetic acid, glycerin etc. All these are heavily used in the chemical industry and thus, their value keeps fluctuating. Chemicals are used in production just as much as metals and keeping an eye on technological and production advances will help you understand this commodity pricing better.

Energy

Energy resources such as gas, oil, petroleum and coal are also traded in the commodities market. They command a high price and keep fluctuating through the day, which makes them good to bet on for a quick investment.

The fluctuation of commodities like energy make the exchange more liquid, which is ideally suited for short-term investments. Creating a separate watch list with commodities that are of interest to you can be very handy here, once again.

Futures

These are known as commodities futures because investors bet on their future prices. They choose to buy them on a particular date and then bet on their value for a future date. This makes futures very similar to options trading, except that futures trading does not always require a down-payment. Instead, full payment can be made in certain cases at the pre-determined time of purchase.

It is important to remember the expiry date for the commodities that you have chosen and settle the deal to ensure that you get possession of it. If you fail to settle the deal, then your deal will stand cancelled and you will lose out on any money that you have paid in advance. If you think the prices have dropped drastically and it is not worth purchasing the commodities, then you can wait for the date to pass by in order to automatically cancel the deal. The benefit here is that if you did not have to make a down-payment you will lose nothing with the cancellation, as you have not yet paid in part or in full. This is one way in which futures trading can be less risky than options trading.

Charts

There are commodity charts that you have to learn to read in order to invest in them. These charts are generally hard to read and you have to put in efforts to understand what the terms and numbers stand for. Once you understand, you will be able to read the charts on a regular basis.

First, you will need to decide what type of chart you want to look at. The most common is a bar chart, which graphs the commodity value over a certain period of time and shows both the average price over a certain period of time, as well as the high and low over a certain time period. This time frame can be anywhere from a minute to a week, or longer. The bar created by the high and low on the chart is where this type gets its name.

Another common type of chart is the candlestick chart. The candlestick represents the same type of data as the bar, but it has an additional feature. It is made up of both a body and a shadow. The body represents the price while the stock market is open and the shadow represents the price while the exchange is closed. This allows you to see the value of a commodity at all times.

Numerous charts exist for every single commodity. While they can be purchased, they are also available for free online on sites such as futures.tradingcharts.com. You will have to look over all the different types of charts to see which kind is the easiest for you to understand and provides all the information you wish to obtain or need.

Factors affecting commodities

There are many factors that govern the prices of commodities and we will look at some of them in this next segment.

Economic factors

The economic policies of a country will determine the prices of some of the commodities such as metals and energy. If the economy is stable then their prices will remain steady, but if the economy is shaky then their prices will also shake.

Factors such as demand and supply, overall pessimism or optimism in a society and strength of currency all play a role. You have to go through the economics page in your local paper to see if there is any news about commodities' prices falling. They will usually clearly mention if there will be a fluctuation in the prices of certain commodities that are used on a regular basis.

If you are dealing with a commodity that isn't local, you will also have to invest time in world news. There are many online resources for this. Forbes and The Wall Street Journal will be of great help. Often the broker you have chosen will also offer daily advice in this department. Being knowledgeable of other cultures and economies is also a plus. If you think what you have bet on is going to see a fall then you can withdraw from it.

Political factors

There can be many political factors as well, which will affect commodity prices. For example, if there is a reelection of the government then it will impact commodity prices. Similarly, if there is unrest or the government has implemented some strict rules and regulations then that will also affect the prices of commodities.

Trading in stocks will require you to pay close attention not only to happenings in your own government, but also in governments throughout the world. Regular news casting sites will be the best resource for you to expand your knowledge base. For other countries, finding a local news site there will give you the best and most up to date information. Obviously if there is a language barrier you need to see if the news site is also available in your language. Many news firms will offer this service. Otherwise Google Translate is always a good option as well. If you know people in other countries who can give you firsthand information, then that is an even better option.

Environmental factors

There can be many environmental factors that affect the prices of commodities. Some of them include natural calamities, rains, droughts etc. If there are heavy rains, then it will affect the perishables. If there is a spell of drought, then it will affect the livestock and so on. Earthquakes can affect energy supply and transportation and oil spills are also notorious for affecting not only oil prices but also other commodities. Commodities that are needed for the transportation or production of other goods generally have a bigger impact on the market then commodities with limited use such as coffee.

All these factors need to be taken into consideration when you wish to invest in commodities. You have to be well informed at all times as not having enough knowledge might cause you to make mistakes.

There can be other factors as well which will affect commodity prices and you have to study them before making an investment. These factors include demographics, trade flow, regulations and speculations. Studies are constantly being conducted on the variance in commodity pricing, as the exact causes are sometimes hard to ascertain. You will not be short of reading material in this department, as new material is always being compiled.

Chapter 8

Mutual Funds and ETFs

The next type of investments are known as mutual funds and ETFs. Both of these are similar in nature yet have a line of distinction between them. Let us look at both individually to understand what each one stands for.

Mutual funds

Mutual funds are those funds where a market expert collects money from investors to pool and invest in the market. He or she will not always specify where the money will be invested as it may depend on whatever looks lucrative at that point in time.

Mutual funds have been around since the late 18th century in Europe, but did not make it to the U.S. until a century later. Mutual funds are not exactly legally definable, but they must be registered with and are regulated by the U.S. Securities and Exchange Commission in the United States. The regulations became strict after the market crash in the 1920s, as the government was trying to find a way to avoid another such a disaster.

Overall there are three types of mutual funds: open-ended and closed-ended, as well as unit investment trusts. With an open-end fund, shares can be bought and sold at any time and in any amount and this is often done directly from the fund instead of from the shareholders. A closed-end fund, on the other hand, only has a set number of shares in the fund and this cannot be expanded upon. This means that you are purchasing from shareholders. A unit investment trust does not have a board of directors, but is rather sold by brokers who have sponsors who compile the fund. UITs also have a fixed life term.

Mutual funds are much preferred by those that are new to investing, as they don't have to do anything towards making the investments. They will only contribute the money and the fund manager will take care of the rest. This means that the time spent in research is a lot less for mutual funds as opposed to stocks or commodities. Often your broker will act as fund manager and update you on pertinent information.

The fund manager will invest the money in many different places such as in stocks, precious metals and bonds. Each investor will be given a unit that is in keeping with the total of every investment they have made. At the end of each trading day the person will be able to check the value of the unit that has been allotted to them.

It is usually possible for people to choose where they want their money to be invested. For example, you can tell your fund manager that you want your money to be invested in stocks alone or forex alone, etc. But once the investments have been made, the investor generally has to wait for at least 3 to 5 years before being able to withdraw the money, depending on the regulations on that specific fund.

It is tough to say how much you can make from your investment, as it will entirely depend on the market conditions. In fact, it is tough to generalize within the same investment lot, as two people holding units from the same batch might experience different results. Because a mutual fund is made up of a variety of investments, the variability factor increases exponentially. Predicting mutual funds can be harder than predicting a single instrument. However, if you chose a mutual fund with a clearly available history, predicting it becomes much easier.

You have to find a good fund manager, who is well experienced and knows where to put your money to help it increase in value. Many experienced investors don't bother to withdraw for 10 to 15 years. Most online brokers such as Fidelity and TD Ameritrade offer investments in mutual funds. They will have a list of mutual funds that have already been put together. You can see what specifically each mutual fund is made up of (stocks, precious metals, etc.) and you can choose any one or ones that you like, but you cannot put together a mutual fund to your own liking.

Mutual funds carry a certain degree of risk as well that you should be aware of while investing in them. You might not always see positive growth alone and must also prepare to witness losses. If at the time of maturity your unit is not doing well then you can choose to remain invested for a little longer to try and reverse the damage to a certain extent.

It is easy to look up the history of a mutual fund and see whether it has performed well and consistently in the past. If you are looking for a long-term investment with steady growth, you can choose a mutual fund that best exhibits this characteristic. Mutual funds are not suitable for short-term investment, as they require a certain time period before they can be sold.

ETFs

ETFs stand for Exchange Traded Funds. They are much like mutual funds but are traded on a daily basis on the stock market. An ETF will be listed on the securities market like a stock. You can buy and sell these like you would stocks. ETFs are therefore preferred to mutual funds for short-term investment. It is like making a mutual fund investment but being able to hold it like a stock.

ETFs are a very recent addition to the market. The first type was offered in 1989, but they did not really take hold until 2000 with the introduction of iShares from Barclays Global Investors. Today the value of ETFs traded in a year is in the trillions.

Those that don't wish to remain invested in mutual funds for a long time and want the chance to withdraw from the investment fast can invest in ETFs. ETFs are also great for those that want to invest just a small sum instead of investing a large chunk.

ETFs generally move very slowly and it will take a long time for it to increase or decrease in value. You don't have to worry about your investment going bad within a short period of time, as that will not happen. Because of this ETFs are suitable for both short and long-term investment. ETFs are generally more tax efficient than other types of stocks and usually carry a low capital gains tax. The pricing is also easy to follow, as they are priced only at certain intervals throughout the day.

As with all the investment options we have talked about so far, you can hold both mutual funds and ETFs at any given point in time to help diversify your portfolio.

Bonds

Bonds refer to stock market investments that are generally considered to be safe bets owing to their reliability. In technicality a bond is a loan given out by you, on which you collect interest. This interest is independent of any fluctuation in the stock market and is part of the reason it is so reliable. Since purchasing a bond means you are lending a company money, you will always be reimbursed before stockholders as part of debt settlement in a bankruptcy process. A bond does not give you any equity in a company.

Bonds are securities where you pay a certain sum to acquire a certificate and then exchange it for the value of the bond at a later date. It is simple enough to understand and an amateur will find it easy to invest in, as it comes with pre-defined and set values.

Here are the types of bonds available in the stock market:

Government bonds

Government bonds have been in existence for centuries. They started out being used in England in the late 17th century to finance a war. Obviously a government bond can be used to finance quite a range of government activities, from welfare programs to space exploration.

Government bonds are probably the safest types of bonds that you can invest in in the stock market. A government bond works on the principle that you contribute a certain amount of money towards the government's fund and they will pay you back the sum along with an interest within a specified period of time. This type is much preferred as it is more reliable and the government almost never defaults on paying back the customers. The only time investing in government bonds might not be a guaranteed profit is during a time of economic upheaval or war.

Municipal bonds

Municipal bonds are a type of government bond that is issued by local or municipal governments, such as states, cities and counties. They are largely used by local governments to fund highway projects, schools and other local government responsibilities. General government bonds, on the other hand, are issued by the federal government. Both types are equally safe and will help you to avail yourself of a good rate of interest. Another benefit of municipal bonds is that they are generally exempt from income tax, both federal and state. The U.S. is the largest issuer of municipal bonds.

Agency bonds

Agency bonds are like government bonds as they are issued by companies that are funded by the government, such as Fannie Mae and Freddie Mac. These types of bonds will also pay a good rate of interest but might not be as trustworthy as government bonds.

Corporate bonds

Corporate bonds refer to those that are floated by corporate companies. These companies might require a sum to fund a project and will seek it from investors willing to invest in the company. Once the project is complete and the company has made back sufficient money, they will repay the money to whoever has contributed it, along with an attached interest. As a bonus, the company might also issue shares to the people as a gesture of gratitude.

Corporate bonds are traded over the counter and only very few of them can be found on an exchange. These are called listed bonds. The only two well developed markets for corporate bonds are in USD and in EUR. You will want to make sure that you research the company you are investing in very carefully. If you are an amateur investor, make sure that the company is well established and has a good history of growth.

There are two different tiers of corporate bonds — high grade and high yield. High grade means that the company issuing the bond has a rating of BBB or higher (up to AAA) and high yield bonds are rated BB and lower. It is important to note that these two tiers of bonds are traded on different platforms.

Zero coupon bonds

Zero coupon bonds are great, as they will tell you exactly how much you will earn from them at a future date. Say for example you bought a bond worth $500 but paid $200 for it. It matures in 2 years' time. Upon maturity, you can exchange the bond for $500. This gives you a profit of $300 over a 2 year period, which more than doubles your original investment. However, remember that it will not pay you an interest on your investment, hence the name, zero coupon bond.

Bonds are safe bets no doubt but they will not pay you well enough to make substantial returns on your investments, as the return is always fixed at a pre-determined rate. You can add them to your portfolio to enhance it, but cannot rely on them to help you maximize your gains. Most bonds will come with a long maturity period and you have to be prepared to wait it out. Although rare, corporate bonds might not be able to pay you an interest owing to their project not succeeding, in which case you would have a complete loss of your investment. Bonds are best if you are looking for a long-term investment opportunity.

Chapter 9

Day Trading and Penny Stocks Basics

There are two types of trades that occur in the stock market, namely day trading and regular trading. We have already discussed many different options of regular trading, so in this chapter we will look at day trading in detail.

What is day trading?

Day trading refers to a situation where the investor buys and sells stocks within the same day. A day trader will very rarely hold onto an asset overnight.

This type of trade is said to be quite risky as the window for error is quite wide. However, it is also one of the best techniques to adopt as you can avail yourself of a quick benefit from your trade. Because of the ability to win big or lose all, day traders are often seen as gamblers by investors. Day trading also requires that you have at least 25% of your traded investments for the day backed up in your bank account.

Day trading has only become popular with the advent of electronic trading. Prior to the use of computers in the trade business, a settlement could take as long as 10 days to be finalized. This would make day trading impossible.

With the slow introduction of technology into the market, day trading was first only available to larger companies and banks. The individual did not have access to a computer at home and so was not able to keep up with the larger companies who were not trading as fast as every minute.

In 1971 the NASDAQ was created, a completely virtual exchange. This further facilitated the creation of the day trader. With the technology bubble in the 1990s, online trading was first introduced to the consumer. A company called K. Aufhauser & Company, Inc., which is now owned by TD Ameritrade, was the first to offer an online broker platform in 1994.

The advance in technology and the ability to instantly trade stocks in real time has also brought with it a new phenomenon called high frequency trading, or HFT. It uses computer generated algorithms to predict when and in what quantities to buy and sell stocks. It is known for trading at an incredibly fast pace with a high turn-around rate. Some say this type of trading contributed to the Flash Crash of the market in 2010 and even though some European countries are considering banning this type of trade, it is still legal at this time. While there is no reason that individuals cannot participate in HFT, most of its participants are business firms.

Because of the risky nature of day trading, it should always be practiced with a stop loss in place. A stop loss is a set point where you decide to pull out from the investment as soon as it reaches a certain low point, or act on an investment as soon as it reaches a certain high point. This will ensure that you don't lose money and can pull out from the investment on time, while at the same time allowing you to buy stocks when they are at the price that you pre-designated. For example, say you bought 100 shares at $2 each. You then choose a stop loss of $1.90 so that you lose just $0.10 per share. Inversely, you can set up a stop order to buy a share that is currently at $1.90 when it reaches

$1.80. This tip is especially important for amateurs to follow, as they need to safeguard their investment. This helps to automate your selling and buying, which is extremely helpful in the fast paced environment of day trading.

Day trading will help you realize a big profit, especially if you pick the right stocks. The best way to pick these stocks is by observing their trend. There will be signs that will tell you if a stock is going to do well and you have to be able to read them successfully.

If you are just a beginner in the day trade business, make sure that you research all stocks you want to buy very thoroughly. It will be best to start with stocks that have a proven track record before you day trade with stocks of fairly unestablished companies.

Types of traders

Swing traders

Swing traders are those that will affix a stop loss. Once the price drops and the stop loss is reached, they will again assume position from the same spot. This is done because they think the stock's value will begin to rise. Swing traders generally buy and sell investments within a period of 1 to 4 days. Because of this, they are looking for stocks that have proven price momentum over a small period of time.

Scalpers

Scalpers are those that will buy and sell a stock within a few minutes or even seconds. They will be waiting for the stock to grow in value and within a few seconds sell it to ring in a profit. This type of trading obtains its profit from the difference between the bid price and the ask price, as often the stock is bought at the bid price and then immediately sold at the ask price for profit. Not all investors view scalp trading as a legitimate technique, while others have used it to great success.

Swingers and Scalpers form the two types of day traders. You will find both institutional day traders (traders working for financial institutions) and retail day traders (traders working privately) on either side of the aisle.

Stock prediction techniques

Stock predictions refer to determining what price a stock will reach after a certain point in time. One line of thinking, called the efficient markets hypothesis, states that the future movement of stocks cannot be predicted, as all its past and current information is already reflected in the current stock price, and only future information, which is unknown, can determine the future stock price. The other line of thinking, however, points out that there have been actual cases of correct prediction based on known facts, so prediction must be possible. Careful analysis of past and current data and information is done to know where the stock is headed and whether it is good to invest in it. Here are the techniques that are followed.

News forecast

News forecast refers to following the news on a regular basis to know which stocks are trending and which are not. You can subscribe to receive a regular newsletter that will inform you about the best stocks to buy. But always remember to do your research on the stocks before investing. Some people also prefer to wait it out after news breaks out to understand the overall sentiment.

There are numerous good resources available to you on the Internet in regard to news forecasting. Some of the most well-known sites include Forbes and Bloomberg. Many regular news stations will also have a secondary business station that deals with this kind of information. Fox News, for example, is affiliated with the Fox Business Network.

Candlesticks

Candlesticks refer to a type of statistical analysis where the highs and lows of a particular stock are calculated in order to find a range. Then mathematical calculations are undertaken to place candlesticks all over the graph and assess the trend that the stock will follow.

We have already discussed candlesticks in regard to commodity charts, but they are useful across the board for most investments. The benefit of the candlestick chart is that it shows both the value of stocks during trading hours and outside of trading hours, giving you a constant knowledge of how your stock is doing.

Fibonacci numbers

Fibonacci numbers are a mathematical tool that are used to predict a series of numbers. The Fibonacci sequence was discovered by Mathematician Leonardo of Pisa in 1201. His formula is still in use today and will help you know the trend that the stocks will take.

Fibonacci sequences can be observed frequently in nature and they also appear in stock trading. They are often able to predict a point at which a stock will reverse its price. You will have to make use of mathematical calculations for this, which might be complex in nature. You can take the help of an expert if you wish to, as many brokers and firms are well versed in this method.

Contrarian methods

Contrarians refer to those that will always go against the general consensus. This means that if everybody else is buying a stock then a contrarian will sell his. If everybody is selling, then a contrarian will buy it.

Being a contrarian is based on the idea that when everyone is saying the market is going up, it is actually saturated and that when everyone is saying the market is going down, it has already reached its low point and is going to rise. While this may seem a bit like reverse psychology, it has been used successfully quite often. You have to be willing to take a risk if you wish to be a contrarian and be prepared for any outcome that might come your way.

These methods form just some of the prediction techniques that you can adopt, but it is not limited to just these. You can study the others, such as the momentum method and mean reversion and implement them for your full benefit.

Penny stocks

Penny stocks refer to those stocks that are priced at $5 or below and typically belong to smaller companies. Such stocks are generally exchanged over the counter as they are not listed on any national exchanges. Penny stocks are popular owing to their volatility. They are ideal day trading investments.

Penny stocks were brought into the limelight by Jordan Belfort, whose life has been popularized through the 2013 Film *The Wolf of Wall Street and* who made millions by trading penny stocks, although he later admitted to and was convicted of fraud.

Penny stocks might not be easy to find and your broker will definitely not encourage you to invest in them owing to the risk involved. Some stockbrokers might also not buy them for you and you might have to do it yourself. There are plenty of online listings of penny stocks available, but due to them not being on an exchange, you need to take extra precaution to make sure the information you are getting is up to date and correct.

It can be a bit tricky to predict penny stock trends as they can move in either direction at a fast pace. This means you will have to be ready to take quick action and ensure that you do right by these stocks. Most analysis you will need to do yourself, as there are generally no charts or statistics available.

Penny stocks can also be pretty illiquid and you might find it tough to dispose of them. Not many people will know about them and so the market for penny stocks will be quite a bit smaller. This can sometimes be a hindrance if you are needing to sell a stock very quickly. For this reason, it is good to already have selling options in place at the time of purchasing.

You will have to look at the buy and sell volume to ensure that you are choosing the right stocks. Remember, penny stocks are only those stocks that are not listed on the exchange. There are also stocks that are listed on the exchange that go for $1.00 or under per stock — these are not regarded as penny stocks.

Adding penny stocks to your portfolio will surely help you diversify it to a large extent. Make sure you stay well informed about the different options available and implement your stop losses wisely.

Chapter 10

Dos and Don'ts of Stock Market

Here are some of the dos and don'ts of stock markets that you have to bear in mind while making your investments.

Dos of stock market trading

Do your research

The first thing is to do ample research on the subject. You have to know what some of the terms stand for and also what you have to do to make successful investments. This book has provided you with a lot of information no doubt but you must not limit yourself to just this. You must read up online and gather more information. You can also turn to other good publications. There is nothing like enough information and the more you read the better. You will also have to buy yourself a basic guide that will teach you to operate the software that you will be using to buy and sell stocks.

You will need to research everything from available broker firms to country economies to current news and electronic trading options. Being well versed in the technology aspect of trading will be a big help to you.

Most brokers have their own proprietary trading software, which means that each software for each broker will differ slightly. Exchanges generally also develop their own software, often called matching engines, so if you are trading on different exchanges you will also see slight differences there. Make sure that you are well versed in the differences so you do not make mistakes when going from one exchange to another.

When accessing the exchanges electronically, there are generally two different systems available to you — the GUI (graphical user interface) and the API (application programming interface). The GUI is an interface that is provided by the exchange and can be downloaded to your computer and the API is your own interface that will communicate with the exchange software. Your own API can be helpful if you are dealing with multiple exchanges and brokers, as it can display all of the information in one centralized place. APIs are often available for purchase from third parties. Unless you are well versed in software development, it is best to purchase an already functioning system, or use the system provided by your broker.

Maintain a journal

Before you get started with your stock market investments, you have to research and find stocks that you think will do well. Look for those that will prove to be lucrative investments in the long run. If you wish to day trade then you can look for penny stocks as they will rise and fall, in value, within a short period of time. You must always maintain a journal that will help you record your day-to-day stock market transactions. You can do this in writing, but an electronic journal is preferable as it can be easily searched for certain stocks or values.

It is also helpful if you keep your research journal separate from your purchase and sale journal. One should be used to track stocks you are interested in, even if you don't own them and the other used to write down all the investment transactions you are making, regardless of the instrument, or whether you are buying or selling.

It is easy to get carried away and many people make the mistake of not keeping track of how much they are spending and where, so a trading ledger will be just as important as a journal. Once again, an electronic ledger is the best option, as it can easily give you the most up to date information without having to do calculations after every single purchase or sale.

It is important to also have a plan in place which will prevent you from over spending. It is a good idea to make a monthly budget for the investments that you will be making in a month and follow it to ensure that you spend wisely. The best budgeting method will be to divide your money up by investment category — a certain amount for stocks, for mutual funds, for precious metals, etc. This ensures that your portfolio remains diversified and that you don't spend all your money in one place and then end up losing your entire investment for the month. An electronic ledger will be the best option for your budget calculations as well.

Employ risk capital

Risk capital refers to money that you are willing to risk. It is capital that you should personally own and must not belong to someone else. Risk capital is also important for those that like taking risks in the market like investing in penny stocks. Remember that the rule for day trading is that you must have 25% of your investments backed up by risk capital. It is best to keep your risk capital in a separate bank account from your other funds. This will keep you from overstepping your budget and completely depleting your resources.

If you borrow the money from someone else and invest it in the market, it is not considered risk capital, because then you will not be confident about your investments and keep wondering if you made a mistake. Therefore, it is vital that you invest money that completely belongs to you and no one else. In most cases it would also be wise to not invest for someone else as they might have different expectations than you do.

Diversify your portfolio

It is extremely important to diversify your portfolio, as has been emphasized throughout this book. You have to have a little of this and that in it so that the risk is diversified. Some people don't realize that putting all their money into the same security will cause their risk to double or even triple, as one simple mistake can lead to the loss of your entire risk capital. Therefore, it is important to invest in stocks, precious metals, foreign exchange, commodities, etc.

At the same time, it is also important to diversify within each of these categories to further diversify the risk. For example, you have to invest in different stocks belonging to different categories such as the agricultural sector, technology sector and energy sector. The same can be done for commodities. An example of a well-diversified portfolio would be the investment in gold, a retail company, a clean energy production company, wheat, coffee and a foreign currency such as the Japanese Yen.

Do take the help of experts

It is a good idea to take the help of an expert. Some people might not be able to invest in the stock market with ease. There will be doubts and insecurities that have to be busted in order to make successful investments. For that, you can take the help of experts that you have in your life. If you know someone who trades in the stock market you may not even have to pay someone to receive advice — all you have to do is look them up and seek their advice. They will be able to assist you with your investments.

Look at how they are trading and the types of stocks that they are picking. They may even allow you to sit in with them on a day of trading. Make sure to take careful notes and answer as many of your questions as possible. Are they holding on to investments for a long time or short selling them? Which exchanges and trading platforms do they use? What is their daily or monthly budget? Do they have a set goal for the return on their investments? These are some of the questions that you should answer.

Don'ts of stock market trading

Here are the different don'ts that you have to bear in mind while making stock market investments.

Don't copy another

While taking advice from someone else is great for gaining more head knowledge, don't copy another person's investment plans as they will differ for each individual. You have to make an individualistic plan for yourself and not merely copy what is working for another person. Even if they are experiencing great success, you have to stick with whatever best suits your investment type.

Remember that each trade and sale has an impact on the market. Even though initially your investing will seem small, it still has an impact. You can look at the pattern used by other people and draw inspiration if you like but it is best to not copy what they are doing as it might not work for you the same way. You can get them to advise you and come up with an investment plan if you like their choices.

It's never a bad idea to run your investment ideas by an expert.

Don't rush into anything

Never rush into a decision, as you will end up making a mistake. Take your time with anything and everything especially if you wish to remain invested for a long time. Be 100% sure about something in order to reap its full benefits. Wait and watch a stock for at least a month before deciding to invest in it. If you are happy with its performance, then invest in it.

This is especially hard to do if you are interested in day trading. The best advice would be to gain some experience in long-term investments first and then keep working downward with your time limit. Even day traders spend hours of time investigating and researching certain stocks that they may end up only owning for a minute or two, but every one of them will tell you that it is well worth the while.

Don't ignore news

Don't ignore news about stocks. You have to go through the newspapers on a daily basis in order to know which stocks are good to invest in and which need to be avoided. You have to assess the market mood by studying the trends. Many people underestimate the value of reading through the suggested stock columns, thinking that it will not work for the masses but it will if you make the right moves.

Never make an investment without at least first reading the day's headlines. This may seem very tedious, but once it becomes a habit you will find it quite enjoyable. Your knowledge base will begin to grow and compound, making it much easier to trade. Remember that investing is not like riding a bike, where you may have not been on a bike for years and then one day get on it and ride it like you never stopped. No, investment knowledge must be maintained. If you step out of day-to-day investing for a year or two, you will need to rebuild your entire knowledge base.

Don't blindly trust message boards

It is not advisable for you to blindly trust message boards, as there might be some bad advice present there. You have to do your own research in order to pick the best stocks for yourself. If you end up trusting another person's suggestions and buy bad stocks then you will start hating the stock market. So be careful when you pick your stocks based on what the message boards have to say about them. Take everything with a grain of salt. Once you have begun investing you will learn that your best advisor is your own gut and intuition that is fueled by knowledge.

Don't be unreasonable

One of the biggest mistakes that investors make is that they remain impatient and expect unreasonable results. This can hamper your plan to remain invested for long. Very few people have become rich overnight and everyone has had to wait a few years before seeing substantial growth in their profits. You too must wait for at least a year before doubling or tripling your investments. Rush it and you might not obtain the desired results.

If you know yourself to be an impatient or spontaneous person, make sure that you have enough guardrails in place to keep you on track. Whether that be a strict budget, dividing up risk capital by investment type, or having an accountability partner such as a spouse, make sure that you take the necessary precautions to avoid rushing into anything without adequate research and knowledge.

These aspects form the various dos and don'ts of the stock market that you have to bear in mind in order to make lucrative investments. Stock trading does not take a rocket scientist, but it does take dedication, patience and perseverance. Investing can bring out the worst or the best in you and it is your choice which wins in the end.

Conclusion

I thank you once again for choosing this book and hope you had a good time reading it. The main aim of this book was to educate you on the basics of the stock market and how you can get started with it at the earliest.

If you have never traded before, approaching the world of stocks can be quite overwhelming. I hope I have broken down all the aspects for you well enough to make the task seem less daunting. You should come away from this read with great pointers for what and what not to do and a book that has helped familiarize you with the different types of investment options, which you can hopefully refer to a friend.

You will find it easy to invest if you follow the steps that are laid out in an orderly fashion. It might be difficult at the beginning, especially if you are suffering losses, but don't give up, as investment will get progressively easier for you, the longer you persevere.

You have to remain invested in a stock for long enough to reap its full benefits. Trying to withdraw from it without allowing it to mature will only cause you to lose on your profits. If after a year or two you are still not seeing the results that you wish, be sure to talk your methods through with an expert. The market is consistently growing and there should be no need to see losses over a long period of time. Stay away from short-term investments until you are comfortable with longer term ones.

This book has provided you with ample information on the topic of stock markets, no doubt, but you must not limit yourself to just this and look at other sources as well. There is plenty of information available on the Internet and you also might find subscriptions to certain publications like Forbes helpful. With modern technology all the information you need for trading is at your grasp, so remember to take full advantage of it. In this day and age, you do not need to be a large bank or investment firm to play a role in the economy of your country and of the world. In investment, anything is possible and the only limitation is yourself.

I thank you once again and wish you luck with your stock endeavors.

www.ingramcontent.com/pod-product-compliance
Lightning Source LLC
Chambersburg PA
CBHW060349190526
45169CB00002B/542